THE
FIRST
PAGE
OF
FEAR
ISLANDS

THE FIRST PAGE
OF
FEAR ISLANDS

By

Aaron Murdoch

Liverpool

Cover Design
Tanvir Ratul

Antivirus Publication
15 Adelaide Place, Liverpool L5 3RJ, England

Antivirus books are distributed by
Antivirus Productions, 88 Shantinagar, Dhaka, Bangladesh.

First edition published in Great Britain
2017 by Lastbench

ISBN 978-1-326-99205-7

A catalogue record for this book is available from
the British Library

Printed in the UK

Contents

1. THE FIRST PAGE OF FEAR ISLANDS

And best of all
I don't even write
My name and my address
On the first page I see

So if it gets stolen
Or my location wanted
Subvert
By the migraines
Bought on by alarm rings

Know that the only cause
Of unwritten books
Is me

Where the samples did not really exist
And had to be forged by a unit of trust
The news today is a test
Of all your friends tolerance

But which will get the message
From that song on anti-censorship?
You will find out who listens to their records
When the sounding stops and confronts
Them for actions

When science is used against me
To say I'm the minority

Then I will acknowledge I am the free one

If you want to see an idiot
Then look at yourselves
When you ask if a Poet
Can be radical?

It sorts out the Poets
From the Record Listeners
It's the source of the heartbreak
When they ask questions
Don't throw yourself into containment

If you get told that would be easier
Why wish to build walls?
And to put obstacles in your path?

That's why I never write
My name or address
On the front page any more
On the very first page

Until stopped.

2. FORGOTTEN IN REMEMBRANCE

So if despised as such
You thought of Nazi's
Why did you hide?
Inside not knowing what's happening?
That set up around us
Everything society now does
Has been learned from them!
Those fought to save us
And we just.. their technology!
Designed to catalogue and monitor
To store on Database
To follow as much as can with cameras
To test out in Belfast
New equipment
I agree we must hate Nazis
But look around
We are letting back in
Their eugenic stink
Through the back door
Letting back in
And for the last time, "Yes!"
And for the only right "Yes!"
It is the same difference
It's always the same difference
Until it becomes a thing
Forgotten in remembrance
Until your fear makes you think something else
How hard is it to back down from fact?

3. THE POSTER

"Mass murderers agree!
  Gun control really works!"
In two thousand and two I first saw that poster
Why I'm unemployed in two thousand thirteen
I saw what it was advertising

It gave me a decade of hurt
And also made you think I was a joke
Subconscious poked discredit
When they told me of freeing consciousness
I didn't think that
Everybody would think like me ten years ago

Those who were not driven by revulsion
Also the deniers and the people put in place
To make sure I went round in circles on purpose
But kept myself impotent
Not having a decade of its scholar
To counter this

More voices to blur in resistance
"Pharmaceutical Industries agrees!
  A generation on ritalin
  Exemption from military
  More money for pills of therapy
  That aren't really helping!"

A hundred percent claims of

What the Doctor's saying
Ritalin generation could grow to suicide
All will be talking to psychiatrists
About how they wanted to be military
But were rejected
And how could that generation resist?
They were introduced to it in a playgroup
And when the oldest child not yet eight years old
Had managed to work out their own class
Teachers
But that was before prescribed Ritalin...

Let me state to historians
I had no part in that
But know I wasn't at the time
Worshipping Queen

"Bloodline dictatorships are so pleased!
  A house of puppets and Sport
  Keeps you on a leash!"

"Ordinary families agree!
  The truth will cause fall outs
  And acrimony!"

4. THE IMMEDIATE IS THE FUTURE OF BARRIERS

A glass barrier on a reception desk
Perhaps frosted glass?
An intercom?
It's more disconnect

I could of reached over
The small barrier
And stroked the chin of the insincere
If I'd leapt over and with fists abusive...

Alarms pounded
I would be removed
Prosecuted
Community is a lie

Your best friends talk about behind backs
It's why I keep things hidden
I know my rights
They wouldn't understand

It was a small practice
On an estate of insignificance
I hope I'm paranoid
But there they were

Taking measurements
For a glass barrier

Across a reception desk
Willing us to smash it

In the red haze split
Is it overrated?
Eye contact?
And the personal touch?

While the Sun is dying
The snow falls hard
Roof reinforced
Go the whole road!

Train Receptionists
In handling small firearms
For self defence
In case the barriers

Are not enough
Against the upset
So you want a cake to eat?
A profession to trust?
Family surgery?

It's either:
Planning for more anarchy
Outsourcing from Hospital security
Or might just maybe

The whims of staff

Who hate it when we breathe?
Measurements for contractors
To build on reception desks

Glass barriers
It's your taxpayers money of course
But does this make you feel
Safer?

5. MADMAN GRANDSTAND

I think the madman is Grandstanding!
Whatever it takes to make you feel
You can handle it
Just to show we all paid attention

A circus trick
Performing for radioactive fish
That is all that is
That isn't to say something horrible
Isn't there

But it's all down to positive thinking
So more debatable than a lie
While a party would insist
I am a fallacy

Time in history proves
I can not be conclusive
But I know one day
When you see this
There will be devastation

So I report on the World's
Beautiful shape
At the time of this page
They say it's the calm
I say they can hold back the storm

A madman grandstanding for snacks
Rise above fear
And then carry on
We've all seen the singers before
If he does not shave head
He will not disappear
But will flock his into joining him
On changing ways to a Christian
And as for the bearded deported
It's his retirement after his Intelligence Five
training
Exposed
And there will be some
Of the singer's fans
That when he mentioned "God"
Turn and run
From the singer in panic danger
Because of that voice in their heads saying
"The singer is wrong! I'm God!"

A dress rehearsal
For the grandstanding madman

6. THE BEING RESPECTFULS

YOU CAN'T EXPECT PRIME MINISTERS
TO BRING THE "FUTURE"
UNDER THEIR ORDERS
WITHOUT EXPECTING EVERYTHING
LESS THAN REVERENCE

So in the future
Always hatred
For British leaders
The spite has kept them alive
It is their birth-right
As much as the Bloodline
Chooses history face
The argument this is a different time
If they occupy their hearts
More than economics
I tell you the hatred
Equals Colonel Gaddafi status
In the eyes of a Libyan
Ordinary and surviving
True at least the British
Have less family murdered

But the venom!
That is in them
Equal level
With some people

London will be Hell on Earth
The saddest thing since hating the frail

Is this hatred will not stop
With just her funeral
Without going for broke
Making hate illegal
Is to make sure
Population dropped
Through deaths
By the time the next
British leader dies

If everyone informed
Then every service picket
And for every other British death
Sorrow and forgiveness

So rob the game!
Make secret grave!
Because some British
Want to sodomise
Leaders remains
With a sceptre
Stolen from a murdered Monarch

When they were asked to pay respects
They reminded them they were beings.

7.   JUST US DUST CALYPSO SCARE

There'll be trouble you've upset their nests
And in short time came to collect
The only chance of amends
Was to pretend nothing happened

This rhythm and it's pulse
Will lose rhythm when you sleep
You'll accent wrong ones
And no longer music
Just words

If you have not the port to this storm
Then anything you have will do
If you have the sentiment
That all it could ever be
Into one object condensed
And was in praise of it
Instead of Satan
Then I will take and drink
To your health needed
Against backdrop
Of ending world

And don't start that again
You will ripple
This particular
Dimension
And the people built on

And shops and buildings
Whole cities
A planet
But not this world

And as of yet no trouble
From the nests occupants
My hand broken
Pulling the bed across
At the start of night-time
To retrieve this pen

And this was how the ink
Rewarded
For saving pen's life:

"NO PUNISHMENTS

NO CONSEQUENCES

BUT NOT JUST
DUST!"

8. ATTEMPTS WHEN NOT MADE MAYBE MORE TERRIFYING THAN ATTEMPTS THAT ACTUALLY KILL

Was that a firing shot?
The only safety equipment
Is to hold it in your hands
Try not to picture
Remember, not an empathic
Just concentrate

On getting the words
Work safe
As it was marked
After charging with its heart
To continue transcribing thoughts

Knowing I could never speak
This well
As could you
In this style
Communicating

Confidential
Competent
Calculating
Collecting
Carelessness

There was a shot

And then that free fall
Now rescued
Safely flown from this
When only one ear works

Passing Bus vehicles
Sound equals foghorn
Air-Raid sirens
Of one note
And just a hissing

And not played at full volume
Just in silence
Always present
It wasn't a plot of me
For firing shots to kill

Where I sleep
But times never change
Here I am
On my knees
On the floor
The beauty is
I've had the victory

Because attempts on your life
When not made
May be more terrifying
Than attempts that
Actually kill.

9. THE STAND UP THAT LOOKS AWAY

So "Deja Vu"
I'm sure a scientific explanation
I support the theory
It's the Earth
Saved from Nuclear devastation
By Alien investors
By forcing it to go
Backwards through time

This means the human race
Is an investment!
How the Hell can you prove it?
For a start...
When it happens
Date and time them in a diary
Notebook
Journal

So HRH Queen
And all are saying old age
There was an international
Arrest warrant
For the Queen over
Missing orphaned children in the sixties
One sole witness
Survived and escaped
To become an alcoholic

If the Queen leaves our seas
On visits or duty precedes
The Queen could get
Arrested!
Wanted for questioning
The oldest trick in the manuscript
Was for guilty to stall for time
Keep this in your memory watching
Breakfast television
A legal document
For our Majesty

An actual arrest warrant
Or there was...
So five o'clock
At anything can happen
The consensus is
I was problem
Until I go back to bed
Time to spot the clues

Make sure there isn't any noises
Have I kept them all awake?
And now exhausted
Sleeping in on the pieces
I haven't stole
From them.

10. ACCORDINGLY ME, ACCORDING TO YOU

And he's left with only
Five sharp twists

Accordingly me, according to you

Preparing everything to last detail
Shows too obviously
An aggressive need to control
A believer
That first impressions are true

Seemingly to me. Foreboding to you

Unguarded is still
The best way to win friendship
I'd only look at the sky
When an eye contact
Problem
Is complained about
Right to my face

Decreasingly to me, leading to you

Eye contact makes me forget
Distracted from values of mine
Digging further front foot down

And it would cost a life
Wasting turning back

Humanely to me, hiding to you

Every turn taken
Has turned to stone behind steps
The sunlight casts shadows
Although not being chased
It is still inside a maze

Swimmingly to me, exceeding to you

And I can hear burning
And the sharpening of blade
One step for oxygen
But this was predicted

Decidedly to me, confiding to you

Enclosed and choices
Instant death
Prolong tension
Or a dead end

Timely to me, rewarding to you

Then awareness
Of being watched by

A stadium full of eyes
But all beholding in silence

Rewarding to me, understanding to you

According to me with accordance for you.

11. ANCIENT STONES OF MENTAL

Whatever you said or even react
It will always be set in stone
As a metaphor
Another accepted agreement
To expose alteration hatred
As hollow of soul

So Bus getting to think of the correct question
They overlook heart of poetry
Was not something mankind could control
But they have invested so much time
Into knocking down again
Hearts feeling full fear

At the very thought of it
They spent so long on preparing
They all forgot to what they were listening
In the first place to
To study invisible stone tablets
To hurl as missiles to the head

Of the person who by mind
Carved into them
And had fired first
By showing them in the daylight
Of an open sunny ancient Colosseum
Even though the world ignored

They were much barbaric times
To the arena enough here are attracted
To sit still
A murmur of people keeping talk
Whispers to loved ones
And there to listen to

New fans
To see whatever you set
On the stones of other people's minds
That were shaped to each individual taste
Of what colour and substance of stone
They would have wanted to have set

Applause after listening to all
The unknown stone setter sketched
And it has travelled all along time
I reach you right here at this moment now.

12. AGENDA 21 IS WHAT IS GOING ON

All of it more was incredible
Everybody needed to know
Which hallowed ones were good
From the charlatan shadows

Flashing between the gaps
In the tall steel fence
That enclosed
For their own good

After being technically felt
Into an artificial guilt
Over a future
They could only be deluded

Into thinking could fight
Shape or change
That distraction fooling
In to all looking away

At the pullers of the strings
And how victory they felt
Over their slaves
When their biggest outcry

Was for when their television
Channel could be taken away

The Jetstream changed direction
To be fired a Sci-Fi that is happening

Across an ocean to be directed
Into full blast Irish isles
And to the land of oppression
That tried to live like it's nickname

Of United Kingdom
Driven from lands and then stacked
In containers large and arranged on
Each of the other with no privacy

Just a thirty foot all for one space
At least they keep the windows
But wherever you are standing
You can't see the tips

Of the tall steel fence
You can't see the child
Who has only turned five
Had a sickness for all her life

But walking outside
And what's left of sunlight
Dances across her eyes
As she runs on dust beside the fence

You can't see from where you sleep
She doesn't know the names

Of anyone arranged
Into stacked containers

Given illusion of mod Cons
And into which herded
Survivors from their ruined plains
But they deserved it

For doing nothing about climate change
Faked
Since records began irrelevance

But say you could?...
That child in this story
Running outside
Your apartment hanging

Say you managed to get through
The tall steel fence
And you stopped the child running
And ask her to take notice
What would you say to her?

"I'm sorry! I believed what was happening
Instead of believing the truth
From executive powers
That marched slowly
Compartmentalised
Thinking they were Holy
The mission to wreck all lands

And send the survivors
Into small cramped compartments
Instead of their seized houses
Lied that this was for the benefit
Of a child just like her
And how we just allowed this..."

13. I ANSWERED YOUR QUESTIONS AND YOU QUESTIONED MY ANSWERS?

"What is your name, and why?"

Because it had been decided
As one of the freedoms
People took for granted back then
I want to grow and live
This tree
That the higher ups
In their control
Want to be made forbidden
And when that status
Ripped from the Earth and destroyed
There is more to the countries than perversion
When you start talking more seriously
And how when alert
The figures all changed
From the schoolchildren
Into adults
My pupils return to the size
Of my previous alert in the quiet
Now isn't the time for you to stop working

"When is my journey?"

To the city that hears me
So I can reward with a silence
In patience waiting to start

And she will have to do the flowers
I still want to protect
So I can watch the tree
It houses birds
In their crucial

"What could they do
That's illegal?"

But in great secret
Their extinction blueprints
Were stamped approval to implement
There is more to this country than judgements
When you stop listening and observe it
There is more to this country than Imperial slaves
When you let other creatures plot your share
There is more to this country than angry young
men
Prejudiced old and the children confused
As to which one they must learn are the rules
There is more to be written but this is ended.

14. IRAQ 1919-2014

I used to write about Iraq
And have it so spot on
I could draw audience member
To tears

I allowed it to get to me
And it soon became bullying
The way I would attack
People who agreed
In the first place

Over a decade later
This pen has turned the page
Iraq
Never say I lost interest

If you remember
I wrote of the puppet strings
And tried to identify puppet masters
To clarify illuminati

When I should have said Globalists
With what I know now
I should of said "Nazi's"
A fascism so strong

All angles blocked and controlled

Only escape route is the lone wolf
Iraq never went away
After everybody washed hands

And from the victors
Changed political parties
And Iraq tried to compete
After Iraqi nationals

That could have made Iraq successful
Were executed after the war
Was declared "Won"
To generate today's events

Eleven years later
This time there will be new dynamic
Both countries population will reject it
A return to an Iraqi war

And those against will never silence
The really stupid who think
That's just what their armies do
And those against

Will be thought heartless
And accused by wretched liberals
Of ignoring the suffering
And despite being proved wrong
The conservatives will instead
Act betrayed at Obama

When they knew at the time
It was going to go this way
But didn't dare say this
Iraq is finally World War III

Never ending
Go out on the streets all you want
The water cannons
Will be sure to wash away

The world got a fraud
The Iraq war
Blood can never be spilt milk
And outside home counties

The rest of the world will accuse you
And Iraq
Damaged beyond cracked
Destroyed forever

A black hole
Sucking everything inside
Until televisions
Everybody ignoring print

Stops talking about what is happening
In all those words
On my poetry works
I've never mentioned

What on the ground
Is happening
So I will say this
Iraq was all our fault

I'm glad at least
For that little time
The people of Iraq
Were able to rebuild

Until it all fell back
Down again
Sparked off
Terrorist incidents
I am sickened by the message
That there must always be a Dictatorship
Ruling over a majority

While countries resources pilfered
The bright side is
The stock collapse in price
But how is that a victory?

Iraq
From other injuries
Has just died
Never making it
To a century.

15. THE DAY AFTER A SUICIDAL THOUGHT

Work out then
Blowing your brains out
A turn of phrase
Caught out of hate

Without considering consequences
And with no regard to how
The other people were feeling
Out of the blue to those

Who had not been following my progress
So really you are going to leave them
Without a list of words
Explaining why?

There were other avenues
And what was the real cause
That beautiful woman who had shut me out
Was right

Telling the truth about
Her French powers
And I was so wrong
Despite foreseeing riot equipment

A pity unpublished as book
What a terrible thing

To shoot head on webcam
And that's not how it's done
Nobody ever sees you do it
Your body is always discovered

But you are dead
That becomes fact
Whoever loved and who discovers
Will live on and see stuff

That will make them think
"If only you were here!"
As much as the thoughts of
Widowed mother and family

And how offensive to people
Who have access to the guns?
So it's just as well
We didn't

Keep this please to remind myself
It is never worth any death by my own hand
But didn't I already write a piece?
Telling me I should live?

Many months before
I was writing this?...

16. THE DRUM CIRCLE GAVE PURPOSE

Don't give the game away too soon
Remember the drum circle
And how your hands hurt
When actually playing them?

This is the actual definition
Of a public park
At the ultimate endorsement
Of a carnival

Always there to remind
And this time never forgotten
The actuality of
Living proof genius

So I returned to the drum circle
And this time played
One two three
Same they were playing

In pattern until
All of the other
Participants
Stopped and had left

Their drums and seats
Violence in my bare hands
Can't get the right ring

Using just palms on the skin

Let it hurt your hands
This is why it's alive
That mastered time keeping
And in all that time

There were still not the tears
That out of logic
Must surely be happening
Against the scared of a butterfly

This is seeing the audience
And still want more of it
Appeared
To it he reformations

Of everything that is supposed to be
In the first and proper place
Let the children blow their noisy toys
To parody actual appearance

And if one Dr. Leaves
Then long to catch us
With how presented
Attended

Oh so he is win
Tinged
Back

Still going

Joined up management of how
Mind find out
The name of the band
"Soundjata"
To explore hopelessly soak
In thesis until forgotten
Where is saying?
I got caught in a Jam session

For the fourth time
And this bought them another moment
On tiger
Thank you for "A" and all it took

Was how it was not U.S but was "You" and
"Us"!
Photographed
Smiling outside
Masonic lodge

Coded for whatever
All signifies final answer
Always was
One two three four

One two three
One two three four five
One to two then three until four

One to three four

Writing in numbers
Now means it's time to
Stop this.

17. THE OUTSIDE EYE SHOWS THE HAPPIEST SIDE

This really has been
The greatest day of my year
It is hardest to see
The future can be improved on

And in controlled bitter scheme of "Reset"
I have finally learned
A style of perfect silence
Knowing that the laughter

Had made it's way up the stairs
And all things could hear this
The things that we do
Back in a moment and the successes
Seems victorious
This balancing act
Has to be done in silence
Even though they are saying "No Problem"

Please remember there's still staying too late
Managed to outlast them all
Despite them just pretending
Conversation carried on

For each others privacy
Everything is all agreed
Things put right

Makes love succeeded

But no-one does that
They all think it's too complicated
From the death that could not sleep
But just stare at reflections of passengers

Water dries the cruellest around lips
With underestimations of the heat
And now from the train station
Their magic trick

Drive into dark tunnel
Passengers vision obscured
Of how City capital turns to hills
Mountains and streams

But they haven't got a joke
To keep the public entertained
And the rattling goes on
As the scenery changed

The dark has gone away
It's now morning
Was it as simple as changing
The ink to a darker on page?
Scribble so quietly
Then pretend you can sleep
Mocking by this heat
Now nobody can run for screaming.

18. SURVIVE THE RESHUFFLE STILL WON'T REBOTTLE THE GENIE

Let it bleed the money in
Keep contained all the children
Let all the guilty go
And then admit there is a storm

That has little you control
All they can report is an achievement
Until all places are revealed
Everyone culpable of secrets

Swept out with a brush
Out of panic
A human scorched Earth policy
Broken pieces of glass

The countries largest
Angriest
And vengeful
Genie...

Everyone pats the leadership
On the back in congratulations
Later that night
After announcements

But the Leadership
No longer can sleep

In their tears on the bed
For tomorrow's headline

The devastation
That had been allowed
To carry on from the past
Just as well the old woman

Who in expensive care had her mind gone
Speaking in a corner
Oblivious it's just herself
Revealing the guilty

Where in her day
You can see why she was murdered
She was so hated all thought it was age
But now with nowhere to run
But to stand still
And get the truth dripped
The scandal of the century
Leaving every too stunned

To bring forward any money
So the fund that contained all the children
Is directed to from the global spotlight
And in the bright and complete reveal

The leadership dusts
The contained children escaped
The Genie got it's revenge.

19. ON THE RUN FEAR FROM UNTIL SAFETY

Exactly as the feared that was suggested mutant
outcome
Laid to rest in one breath and everything put back
to usual
That bare faced lie there was a peacetime let
alone
The latest excuses for war crimes and offensive

To society reflection illusion of what truth spoke
backwards
Using electrical products because live at their
actual location
There is just chaos of ritual sacrifice the electrical
products
Don't remind of sales thanks will never stop for
tanks

And routine checks at station keep it together for
the travel
You know it's not safe now and at worst time to
remember
But I'm telling you cool to just remember what it
feels
To breathe out and relax pause for running
Lo
So eyes not glazed by brainwashing attempts
Directed on physical presence and body against

The always present "What could this possibly
be?"
A steady walk for the escalators best done with

Uncrossed legs for as long as you work out how
that's done
Then pull together the heat comes focusing
A terrible shame criminal thought of in that day
Of times and the charity bowl of level two

Always a spin of what I've become
Despising all who call me by all my name's
Will never if I keep it running always far too late
In the screenplay nobody writing down but from
their

Business plan and yes by now I've said all this
loud
And one person listened so soldier if you think of
it
Logically talk out of punch to stop doing this
On to purpose which is to mistake this is all

A reality does?
A single point of time stretched out into
breathing
Remove keeping cool what disguise is need to
entertain?
And then cat fighting caused and imagined dust

Have I had my hair dressed out of excitement?
Of The Jimi Hendrix Experience soundings?
Mastering exact disguises that the children
From their subconscious had craved in its music

And make generational retort to clap hands eye
contact
Nobody is going to notice what I've previously
just been said
A commentary of the state universal thing
Relate and experience through bought to
attention

With the disregard this heart has to continue
To tell and repeat whilst enough are unconscious
Every connection is valid if I consider my
friendship
A long time waits until asked for this again

Electrical products lost all interest in your fate...

20. DOMINICK HOUSE

Stood outside you
From other pavement before traffic
I pictured the building was alive
And was able to fly away

Flapping it's corridors and floorplan
As wings yet incredibly total silence
The rattling of pens from desk tidy
Heartfelt replacement favourite crockery

All the data stored impregnable
Never wiped despite shuffled in cabinets
But you couldn't fly
You were my Jobcentre building

Trust me wreck up job guaranteed after School
Determined never to claim as the others
Remembers the promise of bridge in allowance
I was able to buy album of Steve Hillage

That I had to get refund as forgot idiot
It was Mother's Day that exact weekend
I have far too many examples
To sit down with them and chart

My progression from unemployment benefit
Through Jobseeker's rebrand
Golden chance of New Deal

And how that turned to mud thanks to them

I remember my sickness
Nobody believed I was depressed
Now I'm closer to finish of my treatment
But I have not forgotten

The manner and footstep traps
Besides how well treated by the day
I miss compiling lists
Of Jobs, references and contacts

To spread across their notebooks
A fiction I had to a pure art!
Dominick House I know of your staff
Who attend poetry open house

Dominick House, does she work still your hours?
Dominick House, I loved your Jobpoints
Far more than padded metal seats
Dominick House, remember my incapacity
appeal?

I had written call to arms of threats to staff
Read back to me word perfect behind strong
glass
The Autumn of ninety-eight I last held the ace
Dominic House, in your own way

You are exertion that influenced my life!

Dominick House, that's why I blank it all out
Dominick House, in truth has nothing for me
Dominick House, to apartments for rent

And I'll carry on my Jobsearch
Until you refuse me
My pension.

21. HELLO SERCO, MURDER CIRCLE

I work for the serpent!
Not the one you worship
Indirectly through Echoes
Sustaining organised religion

And even through work
I have never stared
Into snake's gaze but still took
It's coin to accompany my toil

In my own world I begin to sing
To myself improvised not my collection
Of greatest uncomfortable hits
And even then notice how the serpent

Made me forget my significance of point
Not even directly exposing
The crimes you sneer at the workforce
Of the fast junk made from killing animals

Trying working for the company
With its tentacles in Nuclear weapons
As well simply applying for your forms
All too willing to sign

And if really serpent?
Then where comes the many tentacles?

Loud buzzes
Re-entry planet

Quickly then:
"Hello! You have telephoned
 The Serpent company!
 How can I help you?"

And burn me for reasons
I never tell about the snake
Has tentacles no point in warning
About company as this is why the serpent has
customers

And the rest of the people
Never believe me
And damn that sliver of people
Underground enjoying the ride

Of delusion you could actually join in
Their control because it's forgotten
That a serpent is a company
Not even hybrid it's nature

Is to strike and poison
And it's so large this invests from
Our everyday
To destructive weaponry
And I'm now working for them!
So how do you think I'm feeling?!!

22. REPEATER OF SPACE HERE

The past, present and future
Are happening at the same time
The Moon is older than the Earth
The comet absolved Dinosaur murder

But that means Lizards!
Reptile Archon who geo-engineered humans
This means the reptiles are back in the frame
A copy and right paste click

Our holographic universe is
All hatred but importantly fear
Transmitted to Moon
Around Saturn relay

To feed the hopes of the robed control
Moving chess pieces members of parliament
Start another war

The Princess And The Frog
Was not Disney
Folklore ancient
A description of shapeshifting

Go back further than Pagan
All flags and banners
Upon them an image of serpent

How far you can go

Is how much you can take it
I have read of this
But I'm still not
Levitating

So you want to bore them with Space?
Or collections to summon
Every hidden and catalogued monster
But can't face staring

At monsters on thrones
Open any newspaper
From what could be greater
But currently prison our planet Earth.

23. INTERNAL JUKEBOX IT'S HELL NEVER STOPS

What the songs played internal
Most importantly not of choice
More instincts what insides grab your neck
Keeping insects for amusement of exotic pets

When not concentrating on terminal
Bleep then voice act react
From conversation under attack
Get used to enjoying their awe dying

When exposed they see you
In truth pushing buttons
In another world playing the Bugle
Driving licence and raising funds

The songs play internal from memory
But when ink scratched canvas lingers
Watch how much of language
Is used in collected sequenced worded bolded
pasted newspaper
Advert Television Bus Stop shelter escape to
market
Demonstrated now in your home

Here I am talking to you
And only doing button pressing
In hope of spider web procedure

Catch date of birth
Expiring dates
Last number of telephones

When the songs that had played internal
No longer play out of courtesy
Faceless voices until proved identity
Looking for something else from what I've
offering

And I mean everybody.

24. GRIEVANCE NEIGHBOURHOOD

You looking in too?
Whatever fate truth?

Grievance neighbourhood
Mischievous bayonet gloves

Atlas scale chronicle
Practiced male delusional

Dare you live
Scared to breathe

Decades in
Crushing finger pens

When updated?
Then make it worthwhile

Don't blame me
The scope of failing

I thought having plans
Reported out from the mad

Right or wrong
Tightly done

Provisions cared for
Divisions in word and thought

That word
"Actions"

Click
Belief

Removed child's lungs
Unknown so carried on

Ambulance further away
Rescue plan never made

Harvest of the disallowed
Pardoned lost of missile pile

And built in self-destruct
Cremated faking trust

Microscopic permanent germ
As robotic murderous stare

To bloom into killer
Which room for stalemate

Taken in by softly grin
Raced to dull first place win

Do you know what that's saying?
What of stole accursed daylight?

Beyond a new low for purpose being
Boiling fears when born simmering

That's where you go
Lorry driver hijack
After the date witnessed
Poisonous destructive sayings

"Grievance Neighbourhood
 Reported quiet
 On the years hottest day so far!
 And just several days after the-"

25. LIE ABOUT YOUR ASTRONAUT, VIKING ASSIMILATE

Who said the Viking
Was the only choice
We had to fear
Accept
Employ

What authority imposes?
Castles against wooden horses
Clay huts of thatched roof
Armed enforcement's canisters
Right back to owning huge sword

"This is our power assert!
  Obey and irrelevance
  For your own thoughts!"

How things are now:
Hollow promise
The next dawn sows improved
They always come...
Not just religion

Cattle human business plan
Designed and blueprints
Embellished from Asians
Quite agree mine took part

Shouting out unintentional
Nervous glances on a long walked floor

Viking could attack successful hack
Chipped visor extra gravity
Arms too weighted being hacked
Yet if reversal of advantage

The fight would be in orbit
Viking unable to breathe drifts away lifeless
towards
Earth's climbing Sun.

26. PREDICTION OF DONALD THE HORSE

Ten year stretch
Guts tampered not from spite
Told you long enough
You thought conspiracy nut

Exactly the same reversal
Even with that woman's criminal
Lose every witness proof in statements
Become Prime Minister with an
incomprehensible lead

Whatever gets to climb onto
A plane
Will fly over sharks in ocean
Concentrating on eat

Possible to block the Sun
To reflect plane shadow
To ocean depths
How many accounts calculate how

How long attempts to warn us
For every joke we have
They return with "Have ceasefire!"
Never fails to masonry and Psyche

Crashing down to kill through cracked skulls
The people who never were buried alive

I missed the President
The implicated front-man of dangerous

Wake up?
Don't insult me
Even in school High
Thatcher

When she resigned
I have witnesses
I actually said
"Donald The Horse"

Now save us from Trojan
By taking away freedom

27. A LAST TAPESTRY FOR RESISTANCE

How strange
Devout pain

From the familiar
Stung it appeared

Of Timeline personal
Stopped lying crayon actual

A choice was given
Rejoice dust proven

And see ran to unknown
Cackling at bruise dethroned

In truth unfamiliar
Written tools become memorabilia

More important than standing
Whores deeply protect life broadcasting

Amongst friends
Rubble messages

The best well meant
Protect smiles forever

Prepare receive an old friend

Mixed fair rejection in the crossbreed

Testing of skills hoped never forgotten
Devastating killed trapped befriended from rotten

But had gone without love
For last plan shot down cruel

Into a sleep
Intuitive elite

Despite observing patterns
This stops quick deserving assassins

Of the contraptions
Pardoned culled afterwards

Every solution rolled as movie
Any solutions involved last cruelty

On the back of my hand
One last dash baby skulls

So vivid but still easy to ignore
This rivet uncalled yet still wanting more

When directed in conversation
Dead syndicated on televisions

Compliment disguised

Acknowledged this highest

As interference
Enrapt as serial

Offered but instead
The watchlist fingerprint

Dig heels in further
Grin appeal wins disturb her

Retract into down
Perhaps singleton crowned?

I know what makes it rain!
Peephole dark street to your face

The sound which makes your pen jump
The load too eager to accept stone money

Furthest into attention more
Blood mystery creeps greater swung pendulums

For the ones who of this never used
Drowning the lost for benefit of forever ruling.

THE END